Survival Guide for the First-Year Special Education Teacher

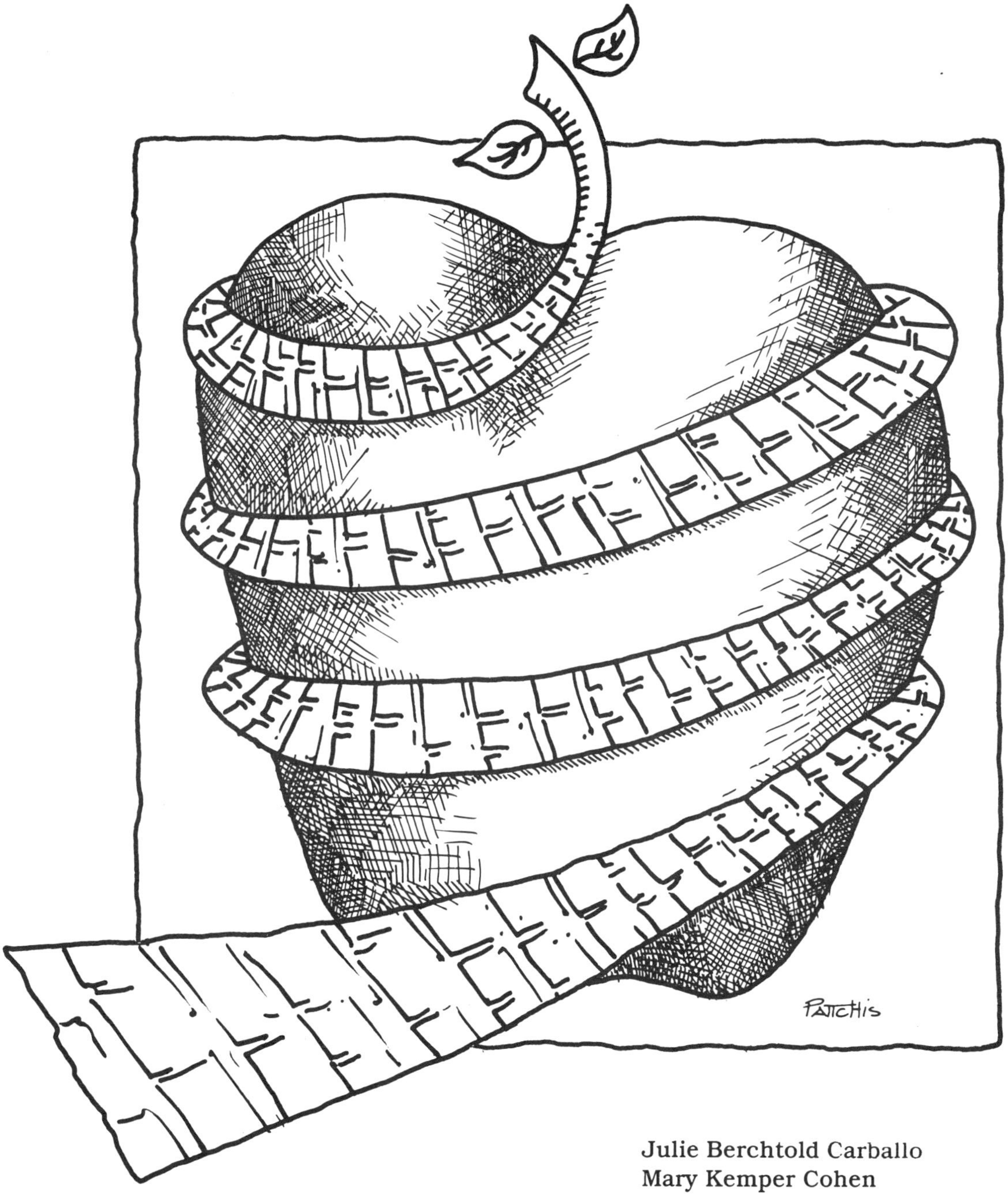

Julie Berchtold Carballo
Mary Kemper Cohen
Barbara Danoff
Maureen Gale
Joyce M. Meyer
Christine-Louise Elizabeth Orton

Published by The Council for Exceptional Children

Library of Congress Cataloging-in-Publication Data

Survival guide for the first-year special education teacher / Julie Berchtold Carballo . . . [et al.].
    p.   cm.
ISBN 0-86586-196-X
  1. Special education teachers—Handbooks, manuals, etc. 2. First year teachers—Handbooks, manuals, etc. 3. Teaching—Handbooks, manuals, etc. I. Carballo, Julie Berchtold.
LC3969.45.S87   1990
371.9—dc20
                                                        90-44609
                                                            CIP

Copyright 1990 by The Council for Exceptional Children, 1920 Association Drive, Reston, Virginia 22091-1589.
Stock No. P335

All rights reserved. No part of this publication may be reproduced, stored in a retrieval system, or transmitted, in any form or by any means, electronic, mechanical, photocopying, recording, or otherwise, without the prior written permission of the copyright owner.

Printed in the United States of America
10 9 8 7 6 5 4 3

Contents

Page

Preface v

About the Authors vii

1. Getting Ready to Teach 1
    Before School Begins
    Organize Your Classroom
    Planning and Record Keeping Strategies

2. Tips for the Classroom 9
    Surviving the First Day
    General Tips to Keep in Mind
    What to Prepare for a Substitute Teacher

3. Building Rapport 21
    Working with Co-Workers
    Working with the Administration
    Working with Parents

4. Interfacing with Regular Educators 27
    Basic Ingredients to a Successful Regular and
        Special Education Partnership
    Implementation of Instruction
    Communication Strategies
    The Do's of Working with Regular Educators
    Where Does the Special Educator Find Support?

5. Be Kind to Yourself and Enjoy 33
    Stress Management Tips for Teachers
    Networking
    Stress in Children
    Practice Positive Stress Management in Your Classroom

6. Think About It 37
    Situations to Think About

7. Some Closing Thoughts 41

Appendix 45
    Information Resources Available from CEC

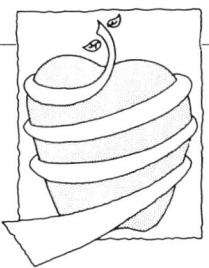

Preface

Toto, I have the feeling we're not in Kansas anymore.
   Judy Garland as Dorothy, The Wizard of Oz

I remember well my first day at a school as a teacher. I was not prepared for how something once so familiar to me was now so strange. After all, hadn't I spent 13 years with over 70 teachers during my own public schooling? But I now was looking at school through a different lens...I was making the transition from being a student to a teacher. It was the first step on a journey in which I am still a traveler.

I have spent 15 years on this journey and consider myself somewhere near my halfway point. When I began my "trip down the yellow brick road," I was not as fortunate as you to have this manual to steady my gait. But like Dorothy and you, I had three trusty companions...the Scarecrow (brains), the Tinman (heart), and the Lion (courage). I would add a few lessons I've learned to the sage advice in this guide.

We are so uncertain about what we know when we first start teaching. It seems as if everything we have learned just doesn't seem to fit in this strange new place. We must remember in our journey from novice to expert teacher that we *do* possess specialized knowledge that we can use to make good decisions about our teaching. We don't ever lose this. The important thing is to "just do it." We'll get better. Remember, the first computer and airplane were really lousy compared to today's models. Our teaching improves as we reflect on and learn from our experience. Use this guide as a journal to record your thoughts on your beginning journey.

You will need to choose your companions wisely. Some of your colleagues will approach their teaching with enthusiasm and creativity. Others will look at only the drudgery and uncertainty of the profession. You will do well to avoid the latter, as they will not encourage innovation on your part. A large part of beginning teaching draws upon your courage. You will need to take risks every day. You must remember that it is okay to fail; but, as author Tom Robbins urges, "fail with wit, grace, and style."

During the start of your journey into teaching, your first faltering steps will be cushioned by the emotions that surround any human endeavor. You have to believe in the worth of every human being, including yourself. You must be sure of your commitment. If you are, you will know zest, joy, pride, tears, frustration, and fun . . . all part of the exhilaration at the heart of teaching.

I welcome you to this wonderful profession, and, by way of this preface, extend an outstretched hand to you to join me on the journey of teaching. I am but one of hundreds of teachers who are there to help you "ease on down the road." You can find us in your school, in local CEC chapters, in graduate classes, and in your community. As long as we are teachers, we will always be on that long walk along the yellow brick road. At various times we will be seeking brains, courage, and heart. Like Dorothy, we will forget that we already have these gifts, and that we have each other.

Using this book as your travel guide and diary, you will make notes about what you have learned, what you did, and what you have felt. Those notes will be there for you to share with next year's beginning teacher. For now, these are my notes to you...from the heart.

Mary-Dean Barringer
1985 CEC Clarissa Hug Teacher of the Year

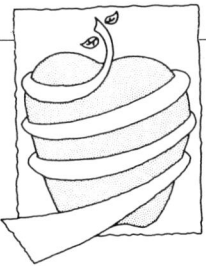

About the Authors

Julie Berchtold Carballo has taught at Argo Community High School, Summit, Illinois, for 5 years. She is the pre-vocational coordinator for 14- to 21-year-olds who are learning disabled, behaviorally disordered, or educable mentally disabled. Ms. Carballo received her bachelor's degree from Loras College, Dubuque, Iowa, and her master's degree in education from the University of Illinois, Chicago.

Mary Kemper Cohen is an 8-year staff member at CEC. She served as coordinator for Student CEC and as Unit Development Manager in the Department of Member and Unit Services. She currently is a Policy Specialist in the Office of Governmental Relations and coordinator of the federally sponsored Clearinghouse for Professions in Special Education. Ms. Cohen previously taught students with educable mental disabilities in a Kentucky high school.

Barbara Danoff is a resource teacher at Georgian Forest Elementary School, Montgomery County Public Schools, Maryland. She teaches kindergarten through 5th-grade students who are learning disabled and/or at risk. Ms. Danoff received a fellowship from the Friends of the Alumni of the University of Maryland, College Park, where she did her undergraduate work and is currently working on her master's degree.

Maureen Gale is a resource lab coordinator for Uruguayan American School, Montevideo, Uruguay. She does program coordinating and testing for students from kindergarten through 12th grade who are learning disabled or gifted and talented. Ms. Gale has her master's degree in emotional disturbance and has begun work on her doctorate. She has taught in resource classrooms and in a psychiatric hospital. Ms. Gale was a Teacher of the Year finalist for the Florida Department of Education for Exceptional Students in 1985 and received the 1982 Outstanding Service Award from the Gatorland Area Chapter. She is a past president of Student CEC and a past chair of the CEC Unit Development Committee.

Joyce M. Meyer teaches children with specific learning disabilities at Thomas Jefferson Junior High School, Waukegan Public Schools, District 60, Waukegan, Illinois. She has also taught in a high school self-contained class for students with behavior disorders and in a cross-categorical elementary school program. Ms. Meyer is working on her master's degree in educational administration. She received the Illinois CEC Federation Dean Hage Award in 1986 for outstanding work as a Student CEC member and currently serves as advisor to the Illinois Student CEC Association.

Christine-Louise Elizabeth Orton teaches high-school mathematics and science to below-grade-level students, 15- to 19-years-old, at Norwood District High School, Peterborough County School System, Ontario. Ms. Orton received her bachelor's degree from Georgia College, Milledgeville, and her master's degree in education from Georgia State University, Atlanta. Ms. Orton was listed in

Who's Who Among Students in American Universities and Colleges and was vice president of programs for Student CEC in 1983–84.

OTHER CONTRIBUTORS

Dawn Carson, teacher of students who are educably mentally disabled, British Columbia.

Eleanor Coffield, teacher of students who are speech impaired, Missouri.

Lynette Flight, teacher of students who are learning disabled, Illinois.

Sue Fox, teacher of students who are behavior disordered and/or learning disabled, Illinois.

Wendy Haight, teacher of students who are learning disabled and/or educably mentally disabled, Michigan.

Bob Hitt, teacher of students who are educably mentally disabled and/or behavior disordered, Missouri.

Clarissa Hug, retired teacher, Illinois.

M. Beth Langley, teacher of students who are multiply disabled, Florida.

Judy Larson, teacher of students who are severely behavior disordered, Washington.

Melissa Moore, teacher of students who are trainably mentally disabled, North Carolina.

Lloyd Nakamura, teacher of students who are gifted and talented, Hawaii.

Kerri Neu, teacher of students who are learning disabled, California.

Theresa Trimm, teacher of students who are emotionally disabled and/or learning disabled, Michigan.

Natalie Ward, teacher of students who are emotionally disabled and/or educably mentally disabled, Florida.

Janet Witte, teacher of students who are educably mentally disabled, Kansas.

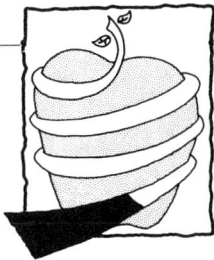

Getting Ready to Teach

Aside from being gainfully employed for the first time in my chosen career, I remember the feeling of freedom and decision-making power I had in setting the directions for my own class. I was planning my own curriculum and program. I was in control and doing the things that I thought were best for my students. Best of all, being new, people expected me to make mistakes and no one questioned or condemned me for my inexperience or inadequacies as a teacher.

Lloyd Nakamura

You've done it! You've completed your initial professional studies, interviewed for several teaching positions, landed a job, and are preparing for your first day. Now what?

BEFORE SCHOOL BEGINS

1. Be confident. The administration has faith in you or they wouldn't have hired you.

2. Remember your philosophy of education. What do you believe about exceptional children and youth and their rights to an appropriate education? About children and their ability to learn? About your strengths as a teacher and how children should be taught? By keeping the answers to these questions in mind, you will make decisions in the classroom with which you are comfortable.

3. Get a school handbook and make sure you know the school's policies and regulations regarding disciplinary action, expectations for behavior, chewing gum, etc. You can bet the students will.

4. Develop a rapport with the principal. Be sure you understand the support—moral, emotional, programmatic, and financial—you can expect from the administration.

5. Have an administrator suggest a fellow faculty member to "show you the ropes" to help you get oriented.

6. Decide what kind of role model you want to be and remain consistent with that decision.

7. Meet with your supervisors; help them get to know you.

8. Try to meet all members of the staff, or if the school is a large one, as many as possible.

9. Get a school calendar for the year.
10. Learn the philosophy of the school and how it meshes with your philosophy and style.
11. Learn about the community that the school serves, particularly resources that might support programs you want to start in your classroom.
12. Take a tour of the school. Where are the restrooms (on each floor)? The faculty lounge? Your mailbox? The cafeteria? Supplies stored? The copy machines? The procedures for checking out equipment? Where is the a.v. equipment stored?
13. Get to know the secretary and custodian. She or he will be able to answer many of your questions. Also, the custodian may be able to help you with adapting equipment in your room and help you out in messy emergency clean-ups.
14. Learn the policies of the state/province and district, regarding both students and teachers.
15. Get to know your teacher aide (if you have one) and discuss how you can best work together.

ORGANIZE YOUR CLASSROOM

1. Make your room attractive.
2. Arrange the furniture and check for needed repairs.
3. Set up learning centers and put up bulletin boards.
4. Find the outlets in your room.
5. Leave space between the seats in the classroom.
6. Make a seating chart and plan to have disruptive students sit near you.
7. Ensure that all classroom areas are free of distractions—store items in closets if possible.
8. Keep working areas free of materials not being used.
9. Check contents of cupboards, shelves, etc., so you know what you have and where materials are stored.
10. Do an inventory of materials and keep it updated.
11. Place carpeting in the classroom, if possible, to reduce noise.
12. Check to be sure all equipment is in good condition.
13. Check room temperature; cold is better than warm to control behavior.
14. Organize your materials and personal teaching supplies.

You have now talked with the administration, met your colleagues, and organized your room. But, before the students arrive, you need to take care of one more very important item—planning. Planning won't prevent poor teaching, but, good teaching will only occur as a result of good planning.

PLANNING AND RECORD KEEPING STRATEGIES

1. Order Materials. Following is a list of suggested materials. This list is not intended to include everything you might need for the first few weeks; it is just the

beginning. Check with the school secretary for procedures regarding the ordering of supplies.

Magic markers	Pens
Writing paper	Index cards
Duplicating paper	Rulers
Ditto masters	Folders
Erasers	Correction fluid
Chalk (white and assorted colors)	File folders
Construction paper	Tape recorder
Crayons	Headphones
Scotch tape	Poster board
Masking tape	Paper clips
Scissors	Cassette tapes
Glue	Fun stickers
Stapler	Cards
Staples	Plastic cups
Pencils	Napkins

It is also important to order a few items that can be used as rewards, such as cereal, cookies, raisins, candy, movies, small prizes, etc. Visit other classes and find out what students are interested in earning.

- Complete a P.O. (purchase order) for local stores and/or a supply company requisition form. Ask your school secretary to explain this procedure to you.
- If appropriate, be sure to include your school's tax-exempt number on all orders.
- Keep a record of what you have ordered and how much you have spent. Give a copy to the school secretary.

2. Plan your first day—and make it creative. Students have probably already been asked to write a paper about "What I did during the summer." For something different, read Judith Viorst's poem, "If I Were in Charge of the World." Ask your students to write what they would do if they were in charge of the school year. This may also give you some ideas about what their interests are and how you might be able to incorporate them into lessons and activities.

3. Plan for the first week—include photocopying materials. Don't forget to plan not only the academic lessons, but also group assignments, social skills activities, and "reward" activities. If possible, consider taking numerous slides of the students during this time. After they are developed, have a slide show accompanied by an appropriate song such as, "Getting to Know You," from "The King and I"; "Ya Got the Right Stuff," by the New Kids on the Block; or some other popular tune.

Be flexible. Lesson plans are not written in stone—you can burn out real quick if you get upset over crossed out, rewritten, or erased plans.

Lynette Flight

---

4. Do long-range planning for the semester and year—What do you hope your students will accomplish this year as a group?

5. Review student files—keep the following information in a case manager's notebook, index card file, or listed on the sample Student Summary Form shown in Figure 1-1. Be sure that you manage student information consistent with district policies. For each student you should have a record of his or her:

   - Assessment information, tests that need to be updated
   - Grade level, past academic achievement
   - IEP Goals
   - Medical problems—allergies, seizures, medications, etc.
   - Behavioral expectations/academic expectations
   - Phone numbers—parents, guardians, emergency
   - Address(es)
   - Any other contacts, such as social workers, counselors, physicians, and/or psychiatrists that you might need to reach during the year
   - IEP review date
   - Student's schedule

   Talk to students' former teachers for suggestions on effective strategies, methods, etc.

6. Begin thinking of strategies for integrating students into regular classes.

7. Plan your daily schedule—to record the times allotted for music, art, P.E., speech, lunch, and any other special programs. Complete your schedule by combining the school needs and the needs of your students. This is a very difficult job, but it feels so good when you've finished it. Be sure to get your principal's approval before finalizing it; the principal may know something you don't. Besides, it's proper to show him or her first. When your schedule has been approved, post it in your room, memorize it, and give a copy to your principal and the school secretary. If you're a resource room teacher, give each of your regular classroom teachers a copy of your schedule, too.

8. Prepare any informal reading inventory or other tests you want to give the first week.

One of my fondest memories of my first year of teaching was finally getting to do what I wanted in MY classroom. Through all my experiences, I had gathered positive ideas that I wanted to use with my own ideas. It had all come together.

Sue Fox

---

9. Plan how you will ascertain the skill levels of your students by using diagnostic tests, teacher observation, and student records. Choose several easy-to-administer tests to use during the first week of school. Ask your new colleagues for suggestions.

10. Gather supplies and materials. Usually to meet the needs of this item you must *beg, borrow,* and *steal.* Most teachers are born scavengers—this is the time to put your instincts to the test. Start with the obvious—other teachers and school or county warehouses. Then, you can continue the search in your own school

Figure 1-1

STUDENT SUMMARY FORM

Name _____ Phone number _____

Address _____ Grade level _____

    I. Reading level and text:

       Units to be covered:

       Skills introduced:

       Vocabulary words:

    II. Math level _____ Chapter _____

       Skills introduced:

       Review:

    III. Spelling and/or writing:

    IV. Behavior:

    V. Available test scores:

    VI. Comments:

    VII: Medical notes:

    VIII. Other contacts:

Figure 1-1

closets, basements, and don't forget to look behind the stage and the locker rooms...famous places for hiding old books. If you are told that there are not materials available, work with your special education coordinator to find resources. Once you've located all of your materials, arrange them according to skill level and subject so that you can easily locate the materials when you need them. You may have to buy some of your own materials and/or spend time making materials for your classroom.

11. Think about your system of behavior management and discipline procedures. Post rules and routines regarding behavior management system, schedules, class procedures (e.g., approaching your desk) and rules. The key is to keep the rules *simple* and review them often!

12. Find out the school's grading system and decide how you will grade.

13. Learn the bus system and the schedule for your students' buses.

14. Make name tags for students (if you are teaching young students).

15. Decide how you will keep track of the students' daily progress. Prepare a form that you are comfortable with to keep daily (hourly) records of your students' accomplishments and problems. These are especially important for teachers working with students who are emotionally handicapped or behaviorally disordered. *Hint*—keep these in a spiral notebook for easy access at all times.

16. Decide which "jobs" the students can help you with.

17. Decide what information about your students you want to keep in your classroom:
    - Birthdays
    - Parent(s) home and business numbers and addresses
    - Medical information
    - Family information
    - Test scores

Now, you're ready for your preplanning checklist.

_____ 1. I ordered my classroom materials.

_____ 2. I filed a copy of the materials I ordered in my records.

_____ 3. I reviewed my students' records and recorded all necessary data.

_____ 4. I have talked with my students' former teachers to gather informal data.

_____ 5. I completed my classroom schedule.

_____ 6. I posted my schedule in my classroom.

_____ 7. I gave a copy of my schedule to my principal.

_____ 8. I am prepared to give assessment tests to my students.

_____ 9. I have located and organized my classroom materials.

_____ 10. I have prepared my lesson plans.

_____ 11. I have prepared my behavior management system.

_____ 12. I have posted my behavior management system in my classroom.

_____ 13. I have prepared my anecdotal record system.

_____ 14. I have arranged my classroom setting and environment.

_____ 15. I'm ready!!!

One of my fondest memories of my first year of teaching was seeing and experiencing each student's successes during the year! It was a great feeling knowing that I had created a successful learning environment.
Kerri Neu

Tips for the Classroom

Teaching goes beyond academics. Understanding and addressing the whole child is an essential of good teaching.

Barbara Danoff

SURVIVING THE FIRST DAY

Be Prepared...and Then Some

The best rule of thumb for successful teaching is to be overly prepared for every lesson, activity, or exercise involving your students. This is especially true the first time you introduce a new topic, idea, or strategy in your classroom. It is better to have more information than you need, more materials than you need, *and* more activities than you need, than it is to have an hour left in the day with no plans. Usually, classroom problems occur during nonstructured times. These types of problems can be avoided with careful planning and some extra thought.

What to Prepare...and Then Some

Following is a list of topics that you should discuss with your students the first day they enter your classroom. A brief explanation follows each topic. Handouts related to each topic should be copied and given to each student as an orientation packet.

> *Getting to Know Each Other.* Introduce yourself and have your students introduce themselves. Each of your students will be as curious about you as you are about them. For some students, an easy way to break the ice is to complete an interest inventory with your students. Figures 2–1 and 2–2 are sample interest inventories. These can be completed by each student and then discussed as a group, *or* the names of the students can be deleted and they can try to guess which inventory matches which classmate. (Be sure to leave your birthday/age off the inventory or you will give it away!) Also, be sure to have enough copies of the interest inventory ahead of time. For students with more severe disabilities, you will need to learn about their interests from spending time with them, their families, and their former teachers.

> *A Place for Everything and Everything in Its Place.* Another important rule for teachers is to *be organized*. Your students will be more comfortable if they know exactly what your expectations are. If you want coats on this shelf, books on this table, and work to be graded in that basket, labels are a helpful idea. Use index cards (preferably different colors) to label these areas in your classroom. If possible, laminate the labels so they will last longer. Give your students a tour of your classroom so that they can identify each area of the classroom with its function. This will enable them to be as organized as you are and more comfortable in the classroom.

Figure 2-1

INTEREST INVENTORY

Name _____

Date _____

1. I like to do these things in school:

2. I think this is what I do best in school:

3. This is what I liked best about my last class (or school):

4. I like to do these things at home:

5. I like these games best:

6. I like stories about:

7. My favorite person is: Because:

8. I have the most fun when I:

9. Have you ever earned money? How?

10. Who would you like to work with in this class?

11. Write the name of a good friend in this class.

12. If you could have a wish, what would it be?

Figure 2-2

INTEREST INVENTORY FOR INTERMEDIATE AND UPPER GRADES

Name _____

Birthdate _____

Age _____

Grade _____

School _____

Sex _____

Date _____

1. When you have an hour or two to spend as you please, what do you like to do?

2. What do you usually do after school, in the evenings, or on weekends?

3. What games do you like to play the best?

4. Do you make things? What things have you made?

5. What tools do you have at home?

6. Do you have pets? What kind?

7. Do you collect things? What?

8. Do you take lessons such as music and dancing? What kind?

9. Do you have hobbies? What kind?

10. Suppose you could have one wish that might come true. What would it be?

11. Are there some things you are afraid of? What are they?

12. How much time do you spend looking at TV?

13. What is your favorite TV program?

14. How much time do you spend listening to the radio?

15. What is your favorite radio program?

16. How often do you go to the movies? What movie did you like the best?

17. What is the best book you have ever read? Name other books you have liked.

18. Name some books of your own that you have at home.

19. Do you like to have someone read to you?

20. Do you go to the public library?

21. What magazines do you read? What comic books?

22. Do you read a newspaper? What parts?

23. What kinds of books do you like best? (For example, books about animals, pilots, stars and planets, etc.)

24. What kind of work do you want to do when you finish school?

25. Have you read books or stories about the kind of work you want to do?

Schedule. The classroom/school schedule should be given to each student as a handout in their orientation packet. Include times for breaks, lunch, each classroom time (subject), activities time, clean-up time, group time, and other important activities of the school day. This schedule should also be posted in the classroom and sent home to parents.

> *My first day, the first hour of school, my class and I were discussing rules for the room. One of my students stood up and stated that he doesn't listen to his parents so why should he listen to any of our rules? I was stumped for a moment. Then I let him come up to the front of the room and be in charge of the discussion and come up with some rules.*
>
> *Lynette Flight*

Behavior Management, Classroom Rules, Rewards, Consequences, and Procedures. The class rules you designed during preplanning should be discussed with the students at this time. If you prefer, determine classroom rules as a group. Review the rules and discuss your expectations with your class. These rules should be posted in your classroom as part of your behavior management system. See Figures 2–3 through 2–6 for sample rules. Try to have as few rules as possible—they will be easier to remember.

Remember—you will need to review these rules again and again. Do not hesitate to review them every day or at the very least every Monday. When your instructors said "be tough in the beginning" they were right! Don't make exceptions to your classroom procedures.

Figure 2-3

SUGGESTED CRITERA FOR EDUCATIONAL POINTS

10-Point Base

1 point	Follows all directions
2 points	Prepares for class by *arriving on time with progress card*
3 points	Is appropriate with *language, behavior, and dress**
1 point	Keeps *hands, feet, and objects* to oneself
3 points	Completes assigned tasks with a grade of C (75%) or better

Rewards

1 point   Completes assigned tasks with a grade of A (94%)

1 point   Completes extra credit assignments with a grade of C (75%) or better

If the base of 10 points has been earned, can leave class 5 minutes early *or* can have 10 minutes of constructive quiet time in the classroom

Consequences

Failure to follow directions:
- 1st time = verbal warning
- 2nd time = 1st check
- 3rd time = 2nd check, 2 checks = loss of 1 point
- Loss of 3 points results in dismissal by teacher request

Dismissal by teacher request = −8 points
Dismissal with assistance = −10 points
Refusal to attend class = −10 points

I have read, understand, and agree to follow the educational point system.

Student Signature _____ Date _____

Teacher Signature _____ Date _____

*Accepted criteria/standards for language, behavior, and dress should be described to the students and posted in the classroom.

Figure 2-4

SUGGESTED GUIDELINES FOR GROUP SOCIAL SKILLS/AFFECTIVE LEARNING ACTIVITIES

1. While the activity is going on, I will not talk without permission.*

2. I will raise my hand if I have something to say or want to ask a question.*

3. I will try to be polite during group.

4. I will try not to disturb others during group.

5. I will not leave group without permission.

6. I will not make noise while rewards are distributed.

Student Signature _____

*Guidelines #1 and #2 should only be necessary in the initial stages of group activities and may be eliminated as the group progresses.

Figure 2-5

SUGGESTED GUIDELINES FOR USE IN DEVELOPING LUNCHROOM RULES

- We talk in quiet voices.
- We talk to the people at our table.
- We keep our mouth closed when food is in it.
- We eat our food...we do not trade food.
- We use our silverware, straws, and milk cartons as they should be used...we don't play with them.
- We stay in our seats except for an emergency.
- We keep our feet off of others and sit in our chairs.
- We clean up after ourselves.
- We sit down outside while waiting for our class.
- We never run in the lunchroom.

Figure 2-6

SUGGESTED CLASSROOM RULES FOR ELEMENTARY SCHOOL STUDENTS

1. Please do not disturb others.
2. Please follow all teacher directions.
3. Please keep your hands and feet to yourself.
4. Please stay in your seat (or area).

Classroom procedures should also be discussed at this time and reviewed as needed. A few examples of procedures are:

1. How to enter and exit the classroom.
2. How to ask for assistance.
3. How to turn in completed work.
4. How to earn extra points.
5. How to get a drink of water, request to use the restroom, sharpen pencil, earn free time, rewards, etc.
6. What happens if a rule is broken.

One situation I encountered for which I didn't feel adequately prepared was how to handle discipline problems with students who were emotionally or behavior disordered and other lower functioning individuals. I handled the situation by observing other classes, reading journal articles, etc. I then devised my own discipline procedures for each individual student. Individualization was the key—no two students can be handled alike.

Melissa Moore

Assignments. During preplanning you prepared several easy-to-administer diagnostic tests that were either commercial or teacher-made. These tests may be administered during your first day or sometime during the first week of class. However, the sooner you administer these tests, the sooner you can match each student to the appropriate academic textbooks. This type of immediate structure is helpful in establishing a smooth running classroom. Testing also breaks up the "too many rules in one day" syndrome, and it gives you a chance to observe your new students at work on a task. (Of course, you have your anecdotal records ready for notes because you prepared them during preplanning.) If time allows, prepare an easy quiz. It will give the students a chance to earn a good "first" grade.

Social Skills/Affective Learning. Obviously, if you've been explaining rules and procedures all day, you've conducted social skills and affective training the entire day. Surprised? Here are a few ideas to start you off for your first week of group activities. Normally, it is not necessary to begin group activities of this type the first week, but there are always exceptions. It's up to you and your supervisor to work out when you should begin social skills and affective work with your students.

Ideas for Group Activities

1. Self-evaluation of behavior—Students can complete Figure 2-7 before or during group and discuss their answers. They can also pinpoint personal goals related to the classroom, and display these goals in the room.
2. What is confidentiality? Why is it important?
3. Review points earned and problem areas for the day; discuss positive growth and areas to improve.
4. Discuss special education—what it is, why each student is in your class, and what their goals are.
5. Weekly wrap-up—How did they do?

Going Home or *We Made It Through the First Day!* This is the time for you to congratulate your students (and yourself) upon completing the first day of school. Distribute any homework assignments, introductory letters to parents, emergency cards, point cards, permission slips, coats, hats, etc. Be sure to help students find the right bus and/or their parents.

P.S. This is not Gone With the Wind. If you want tomorrow to be as positive as today, you better think about it *now*—not tomorrow. So wave good-bye to your students and get back in the classroom and start planning for tomorrow. Review what went right and what went wrong and plan accordingly. (Don't be shy—seek out veteran teachers for helpful suggestions.)

Do not try to be friends with students at first. Establishing myself as an authority figure gained my students' friendship.

Sue Fox

A Final First Day Checklist

____ 1. I have made copies of the schedule for my students.

____ 2. I have made copies of the interest inventory that I want to use.

____ 3. I have labeled the necessary areas in my classroom.

____ 4. I have made copies of my behavior management system for my students (class rules, rewards, consequences, and procedures).

____ 5. My assignments for the day are copied and organized.

____ 6. My topic for group social skills is decided and my handouts (if any) are copied.

____ 7. I know exactly what I'm going to say and do my first day with my students.

____ 8. I will reward my students (and myself).

____ 9. I will plan for tomorrow *today*.

____ 10. I'm ready! (Good luck!)

Figure 2-7

SELF-EVALUATION OF BEHAVIOR

Name _____

Date _____

MY SCHOOL BEHAVIOR:

	Always	Sometimes	Never
1. Do I get to class on time?	1	2	3
2. Do I bring necessary materials to class?	1	2	3
3. Am I a good listener?	1	2	3
4. Am I quiet and orderly in the lunch line?	1	2	3
5. Do I use good lunchroom manners?	1	2	3
6. Am I quiet when changing classes?	1	2	3
7. Do I help keep the school clean and neat?	1	2	3
8. Do I follow directions?	1	2	3
9. Do I talk at appropriate times?	1	2	3
10. Am I polite to others?	1	2	3

I need to work on these things:

GENERAL TIPS TO KEEP IN MIND

1. Try to spend some time with each student one-on-one in the first few weeks to get to know them as individuals.
2. Don't start a new lesson on Friday—most likely, the students will not remember it on Monday.
3. Move around the room—don't sit at your desk for extended periods of time.
4. Don't be afraid to ask for help—you aren't expected to know everything. There are plenty of resource people around (i.e., other teachers, both special education and regular education, counselors, therapists, librarians) who will be happy to help. Use them.
5. Bring your sense of humor to your teaching—it is one of your best tools.
6. Bring a favorite snack (your reward).
7. Confront behavioral problems immediately.

An important lesson I learned was to establish control of my students and let them know what I expected. Set high expectations and your students will succeed.

Kerri Neu

8. Do not discuss your students in the teacher's lounge; always be positive about your special children.
9. Keep a positive attitude around students *and* adults.
10. Don't take your school home and don't take your home to school.
11. Write a letter about your first day to a favorite professor, your mom, or a CEC pal.
12. Do not expect to be told you did a great job.
13. Make friends with the cafeteria workers, custodians, and secretaries—they are important friends to have.
14. It's far more important to be fair and firm than it is to be liked. And, if you do the former, the latter will follow.
15. Stay organized—it helps more than you will realize.
16. When possible, observe other teachers and their rooms.
17. Establish routines for yourself and for the students.
18. Keep records up-to-date.
19. Learn which materials are effective for use with which students and also which skills the materials strengthen.
20. Avoid "syndromes": The Messiah syndrome—"I will save you" (it lasts until the holidays); the "I am incompetent" syndrome (it lasts until spring break); followed by the "These kids are hopeless" syndrome. Remain positive and expect to have some bad days.
21. Celebrate learning!

WHAT TO PREPARE FOR A SUBSTITUTE TEACHER

You wake up one morning and realize, "Uh-oh! I am too sick to go to school today. But, a substitute won't know about Bill's special reading assignment, or Jessica's individual work. I guess I'll have to go to school."

Just as you need to be prepared for your students, you also need to be prepared for a substitute teacher. Take time to prepare a "substitute teacher" folder, so that when you are too sick to go to school, everything will be in place for a substitute.

Keep the substitute teacher's file on your desk and place items in it that would introduce the substitute to your students, your classroom, your routine, your behavior management system, etc.

Items to Include in a Substitute Teacher's File

1. Your schedule.
2. If the school is large, a map of the school.
3. A teacher to contact in case of questions, emergencies, etc.

4. Procedures for fire drills, storm warnings, etc.
5. Schedules for teacher aides.
6. A list of your students, including their schedules with you, any special considerations, behaviors, medical problems, and, finally, who is reliable.
7. An overview of classroom procedures, rules, record keeping, etc.
8. Location of materials and rewards.
9. Directions for use of free time.
10. Special teaching procedures or activities.
11. Tips for helping the substitute work with your students—any strategies you've found effective that may come in handy.
12. A feedback form for the substitute to complete containing information about student attendance, behavior, work that was completed, other comments, etc.

Review the folder occasionally to make sure its contents and comments are accurate. Your schedule and/or your tips about the students may change during the year.

Positive Reinforcers

Take roll
Leader in line
Free time in the media center
Trip to an ice cream parlor
Can blow a bubble in class
Pounding on the desk for 30 seconds with hand
Make funny faces at the teacher
Visit the library
Write on the board
Ten seconds of applause
Message to a friend
Fifteen minutes to sit quietly under a tree
Chew gum at lunch
Music in the classroom
Howling for 30 seconds
Lunch outside
Teacher carries books
Free popcorn and old movies
Boo for 10 seconds
Tell a fairy tale
Tell funny incident in his or her life
Class pantomimes
Listen to a Bill Cosby record
Do a one-person TV commercial
Make up a funny song
Sing a funny song
Class tries to make student laugh in 10 seconds

Pretend you are a one-person band
No homework
Paper ball thrown at garbage can
Close windows in the afternoon
Read a comic book or newspaper
Teacher buys/serves the student's lunch
Popping balloons in class
Free period of creative activity
Tell a joke
Free period to play records
Phone call of approval to home
Teacher shakes everyone's hands enthusiastically
Pass to visit a fast food restaurant
Award an "I'm Special" certificate
Candy
Make and throw a paper airplane
Individual game
Arm-wrestle the teacher
Three minutes early to lunch
Coin football or hockey
Teacher buys a coke for student
Clothes swap
Teacher eats with students
Ghost stories with no lights on
Tap dance
Wear a paper bag
Write on the board

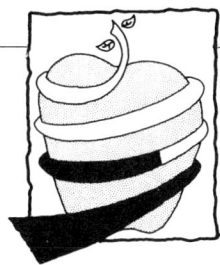

Building Rapport

One of the most important lessons I learned during my first year of teaching is the importance of teamwork and cooperation. Working together with your colleagues is important, especially for special education teachers. Education is a collaborative effort and no matter how good a teacher you are, you can't be effective without help. Sometimes working with veteran teachers can be frustrating (especially if they don't have any special education training). There were many times when I had to 'bite my tongue' and compromise because I realized that somewhere down the line, I would need the cooperation of that other teacher.

Lloyd Nakamura

WORKING WITH CO-WORKERS

1. Make it your business to get along with your co-workers.
2. Let introductions move along naturally; be personable.
3. Talk about positives and avoid negatives.
   - Don't spend time criticizing.
   - Accept different opinions and suggestions.
4. Ask co-workers for advice/suggestions; it helps you out and makes them feel helpful.
5. Offer to help others.
6. Be a part of school activities (i.e., faculty luncheons, chaperoning, informal parties, staff committees, etc.).
7. Don't try to meet everyone at once.

Breaking the Ice and Getting to Know Your Co-workers

Here are a few tips that may make this easier:

- Don't alienate your new colleagues by criticizing the way daily routines are handled.
- Don't constantly say, "At the school where I used to work (or student taught) we

did it this way...." (There is nothing more annoying than someone who comes to a new place and tries to change everything overnight, or who thinks that the place he or she used to work had the best way of doing something.)

- Do ask a few teachers (separately) to help you solve a problem. (Everyone loves to be asked for advice.)
- Do try to cultivate one friendship at a time, rather than taking on the whole crowd at once.
- Don't give up. After you get to know them, and they get to know you, you'll probably wonder why you felt so intimidated or frustrated.
- Have patience—you are the new one, not them.
- Prioritize the most important goals of your program and choose your issue carefully before you try to fight an established policy or a fellow teacher, parent, or administrator.
- Remember, you are still learning.

WORKING WITH THE ADMINISTRATION

Everyday dealings with the administration are important to you. Here are a few tips you can use to make the right impression.

1. Ask questions—be sure you know what is expected of you as a teacher with regard to responsibilities, duties, and extracurricular positions or activities.
2. Ask your administrator to suggest a specific person to help you.
3. Pay attention and learn overall organizational activities. Also attend meetings (i.e., faculty, school board, PTA).
4. Never gossip or become involved in small talk concerning your administration.
5. Be open to constructive criticism, advice, and suggestions.
6. Be cooperative and respect opinions.
7. Ask about all policies and know proper procedures with regard to dealing with students and parents. Find out how to record parent conferences.
8. Let the administration be aware of special situations with students and parents.
9. Be prompt and efficient.
10. Deal with discipline problems as much as possible on your own. If you use the principal as little as possible, it gives both the principal and you more confidence in your abilities.
11. Realize that your administrator believes that you are qualified for the job—be confident!
12. Be optimistic, show your respect, be cooperative and flexible, and your job will be much more enjoyable.
13. Be sure you understand the district's teacher evaluation program.

WORKING WITH PARENTS

1. Always be professional!
2. Strive for clear, consistent communication:

- Be honest and sensitive.
- Be precise.
- Let problems be known and, when appropriate, organize a conference to discuss the problem. Keep summaries of conferences on file.
- Stress the positives.
- Work together.
- When appropriate, ask suggestions of the parents. They know their child best.
- Don't use special education jargon; talk in terms they can easily understand.

> *Keep in close contact with parents. Notes, phone calls, visits are great. Invite them to visit. Kill them with kindness—even the reluctant or uncooperative parents cannot resist a smile and a positive attitude.*
>
> Wendy Haight

3. Conduct effective parent conferences.* Parent conferences provide an opportunity for parents and teachers to share information and ideas with the goal of improving the student's learning experience. Use the following list of tips and techniques to help improve the quality of your meetings with parents. (Refer to Figure 3–1 for a list of words and phrases that can be used when communicating with parents.)

   - Schedule parent conferences carefully. Do not schedule too many conferences in one day, especially with parents of students who are not doing well.
   - Make sure your parent-conference schedule is convenient for working parents.
   - Put a few chairs in the hall so parents can be comfortable while they wait for their conference.
   - Post your daily conference schedule on the door. Stay on schedule. If a parent arrives late and it will throw off your schedule, reschedule the conference. If you want to schedule a break for yourself, write it on the schedule as a "meeting" and go relax during that break.
   - Conduct conferences at a table instead of from behind your desk. (This will be more informal and, therefore, less threatening to parents.) Provide note paper and pens so parents can write down information. Keep note paper handy for writing down information you want to remember, too.

> *When identifying students with learning disabilities, I found it very difficult to tell parents that their child is handicapped. To deal with this situation, I talked the issue over with my principal and read some research. I then made a packet and book list for parents to help explain learning disabilities. I also provided parent workshops that address their concerns.*
>
> Barbara Danoff

---

*Note. From *Managing Your Classroom* (pp. 28–33) by B. Gruber, 1983, Torrance, CA: Frank Schaffer Publications, Inc. Adapted by permission.

Figure 3-1

COMMUNICATE CLEARLY WITH PARENTS ON REPORT CARDS AND CONFERENCE FORMS

Make a list of words and phrases to use on parent conference forms, report cards, and notes to parents. Add your own ideas to the following list of suggested comments.

Positive Comments:

- off to a good start
- high level of self-esteem
- wants to do well
- willing to work hard
- responds well to praise and/or constructive criticism
- accepts responsibility
- self-motivated
- is a leader
- at top of group
- having a good year
- enthusiastic
- all-around good student
- creative
- working at grade level
- mature
- confident
- eager to please
- grasps new concepts quickly
- has many friends
- doing well in all academic subjects
- sets high standards
- self-starter
- helpful to others
- at top of class
- takes pride in work
- high interest level
- cooperative
- especially talented in...
- pleased with progress
- enthusiastic about learning

Not-So-Positive Comments:

- inattentive
- fine motor difficulties
- slow completing work
- hard-to-discipline
- has difficulty verbalizing
- unpredictable
- impatient
- has difficulty following oral directions
- has difficulty with (subject)
- has difficulty organizing and planning work
- unable to work with others
- easily frustrated
- disturbs others
- demands too much attention
- talking interferes with work
- seems unsure of self
- depends on rote learning
- displays lack of interest
- dependent behavior
- has not developed problem-solving skills
- overactive
- gross motor difficulties
- does not complete work
- short attention span
- has difficulty concentrating
- defiant
- overly sensitive
- has difficulty following written directions
- tends to daydream
- has difficulty concentrating on schoolwork
- teases other children
- has difficulty keeping up with group
- has difficulty working independently
- easily distracted by others
- unable to maintain friendship(s)
- resorts to show-off behavior
- poor work habits hinder progress
- displays lack of motivation
- easily influenced by peers

- Stay on the subject; if the parent digresses, it is your responsibility to get the conference back on track.
- If a conference does not go smoothly, schedule another meeting with the parents. You may want to ask the principal to attend this second conference.
- Keep a record of what you discuss with the parents.
- Student records are available to parents as legislated in the Family Rights and Privacy Act of 1974. If parents want to see school records or add information to records, refer them to your administrator. Know your district's policy.
- Write a list of things parents can do to help their children at home. Duplicate your list and give it to parents during the conference. Be careful, though, with what you suggest parents work on at home with their children. Try to suggest activities that complement their schedules rather than require parents to reorganize to make time for complex programs.
- Keep parents informed throughout the school year. When parents know what is happening at school, conferences can be more productive. Well-informed parents tend to feel more positive about the school, too.
- Be cautious about suggesting specific tutors, learning clinics, family counseling centers, special diets or medications, or other professional services. Instead, you might ask the parent "have you considered seeking outside help for the child such as...?" Recommendation of a specific outside service could make the school district responsible, especially if that service proves to be unsatisfactory. Be sure you know district policies and procedures in this regard.
- Keep a record of the conferences you have with parents. Also, write down any phone calls or incidental, at-the-door conferences.
- Keep an anecdotal record for your students. This record will come in handy during parent meetings, when writing special requests, and when explaining problems to a school nurse, counselor, or administrator.
- Don't compare one child to another.
- Try to see things from the parents' point of view.
- Be sure parents know that you care and that you have a sincere interest in their child's personal and educational growth.
- End the conference on a positive note.

4. Follow-up on conferences. Put into action the treatment necessary to remediate the problem. Ask parents to keep the communication lines open and stay in contact.

5. Maintain communication with parents and keep records of all communication. Make use of letters, phone calls, special notices, and conferences as needed.

An important lesson I learned during my first year of teaching was that change takes time, not just in students but also in school policies and attitudes. Caring about the students is what is most important.

Bob Hitt

Parents are the most important influence a child can have. Each home is unique; each child is unique. There are no absolute answers, but there are some things that you can do to make life easier. If asked, share suggestions with the parent for working with the child. Some examples of hints for parents are:

1. Be understanding of your child.
2. Praise your child daily for the little things he does well.
3. Do not compare your child's achievements to other children her age.
4. It is essential that children learn that it is more important to compete against themselves than against others.
5. Establish firm rules and structured routines, including regular mealtimes and early bedtimes!
6. Give your child household chores and responsibilities.
7. Watch for signs of anger when your child comes home from school. He may have had a rough day.
8. Please watch your child's diet; avoid excessive sweets.

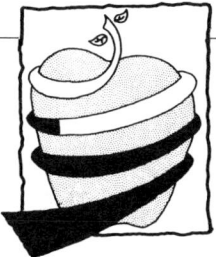

Interfacing with Regular Educators

College does not fully prepare you for everything. Don't be afraid or ashamed to ask for help or advice from fellow teachers. They are willing to help.

Melissa Moore

4

Regardless of whether you are teaching in an elementary, middle, high school, or special center, it will be important for you to establish cooperative working relationships with the regular education teachers. With the passage of P.L. 94–142, this cooperative working relationship took on additional importance—students with disabilities are taught in the regular classroom as much as possible. As a teacher trained to work with special needs students, you may also find yourself needing to assist regular educators who have mainstreamed students in their classrooms.

BASIC INGREDIENTS TO A SUCCESSFUL REGULAR AND SPECIAL EDUCATION PARTNERSHIP

1. Be flexible.
2. Get involved as much as possible in school activities, such as the P.T.A., student council, social committee, assemblies, and school in-service programs.
3. Get to know each teacher's style, classroom procedures, strengths, and needs. Understand and respect the content or subject matter expertise that these teachers have. Their knowledge can greatly complement your work.
4. Work harder than you are expected to. Teachers need to build a positive attitude toward the specialist position. Help them in any way possible.
5. Accentuate the positive: Tell teachers what they're **already** doing well and why it works. Remember to say, "Thank you!"
6. Remember that everyone has the same goal: to help children learn.
7. Remember that the special needs student may be an unknown challenge to regular teachers and the unknown can be frightening. Help them to become comfortable with exceptional students.

IMPLEMENTATION OF INSTRUCTION

Since most exceptional students spend part or most of their day in regular education, it is important that you coordinate your instructional program with that of your regular education colleagues. Although this collaborative effort may have many different names, there are some essential conditions necessary for it to be successful.

1. The relationship must be voluntary. Get to know your regular education colleagues so that you will want to work together.
2. The relationship must be built on mutual respect for each other's expertise—together you can help the student.
3. Both of you should work together on common goals for the child.
4. Both of you should be willing to share responsibility and accountability for achieving those goals.

Following are three common collaborative approaches:

1. **Team teaching**: Both the regular and special educator teach the same instructional objectives with modifications for exceptional students. Modifications include additional use of manipulatives, assignment modifications, small group instruction, and individualized instruction or enrichment.
2. **Common curriculum instruction**: The special educator and classroom teacher simultaneously teach different instructional levels. Each professional teaches the curriculum skills, but the special educator modifies instruction to the individual needs of the students.
3. **Supplemental skills development**: Exceptional students receive classroom instruction and remedial assistance concurrently. The special educator provides the students with supplementary instruction based on skills necessary to function on grade level.

When a student is in need of one of these strategies, it will be necessary to meet with the regular class teacher, parent, and other professionals involved in the child's academic program. This can be intimidating to regular educators (and the parents if they are included). Following are some suggestions to help the regular educator feel more comfortable.

COMMUNICATION STRATEGIES

Before the Meeting Begins

1. Set a schedule for the meeting highlighting major topics and/or points to discuss and review this briefly with the teacher.
2. Remind the classroom teacher to bring the student's work samples in the area of concern.
3. Arrange for refreshments (coffee, water, etc.).

During the Meeting

1. Introduce the classroom teacher to everyone at the meeting.
2. Have the classroom teacher sit next to you.
3. When an academic area is a concern, ask questions to probe for further understanding of the exact concern.
4. Make suggestions to assist the classroom teacher when working with the student. He or she should be able to go back to the classroom with constructive teaching approaches, accommodations, and/or modifications.

5. Immediately write down on a "things to do" list any responsibilities for which you are accountable.

6. When wrapping up the meeting, directly ask the teacher, "Can we help you in any other way?" or "Do you feel comfortable with the recommendations?"

After the Meeting

1. Provide the classroom teacher with a copy of the meeting notes.

2. Follow through on promises!

3. Check with the teacher a week or so after the meeting to offer further assistance.

When special education students are in the regular classroom it is important to monitor student behavior and workload on a regular basis. The special educator needs to act as an advocate for students while supporting the regular educator. In order to support the regular educator, good communication is needed.

> *Dealing with the politics of the school forced me to be a mediator, salesman, diplomat, and negotiator. Everyone in the school—teachers, administrators, parents, support staff, et al.—has a job to do and they are all trying to protect the interests of the students they serve in the context of their own situation. How was I going to push my own agenda in order to do the best possible job for my students? My involvement in CEC really helped me with this situation. It took a lot of give and take. I sat down and communicated my concerns to the others and listened earnestly as they expressed their views to me.*
>
> Lloyd Nakamura

To build ongoing communication with the regular classroom teacher:

1. Emphasize the positive attributes of students and the benefits of including them in a regular classroom.

2. Develop each student's program with the classroom teacher.

3. Provide support through team teaching, making modifications, and reinforcing students and teachers.

4. Be flexible.

5. Set dates to evaluate each program and each student's progress. Keep to that schedule.

6. Modify the program if necessary.

7. If possible, coordinate your planning time with the classroom teacher, especially if you are team teaching. Schedule a regular time to meet.

8. Before and after school "check in" and ask how things are going. Don't forget the "things to do" list. By the end of your rounds the list will surely be filled.

9. Have an open door policy for your room. One way to encourage teachers to drop by is to have a fresh pot of coffee (or a jar of M & M's), then just spread the news!

10. Assist teachers in developing alternate teaching strategies for working with exceptional students.

11. Communicate in writing when necessary. For students who see many adults during a school day (such as a classroom teacher, resource teacher, speech therapist, volunteer) a communication sheet is helpful.

    - Provide the student with a folder and staple the communication sheet in it.
    - Encourage each professional to note what the student worked on during the session, the objective mastered, and what needs to be reviewed.

THE DO'S OF WORKING WITH REGULAR EDUCATORS

1. Implement instruction that directly correlates to classroom curriculum.

2. Keep a "things to do" list close at hand. Write down ideas, teacher requests, etc. This will promote organization!

3. Make time for collaboration.

4. Know that the following may be resources you can use.

    - Peer tutors
    - Senior citizen volunteers
    - University students
    - P.T.A.

    All of these individuals can work with mainstreamed students in the classroom. This offers the regular educator extra support.

5. Demonstrate "positive talk" when discussing students. Remember the rule of confidentiality when talking with teachers.

6. When suggesting accommodations to the regular educator try to model the program and/or modification. Have the teacher observe how to use the accommodation appropriately before expecting him or her to use it.

7. Suggest modifications that can be implemented with a group of students, such as on-task reinforcement and manipulative materials.

8. When working in the regular education classroom, follow the teacher's class rules. This provides the students with consistency and allows teacher teamwork to begin.

9. Give each teacher a copy of your schedule so each one will know where to locate you.

10. Ask regular educators for advice and suggestions. Bouncing ideas back and forth often provides a partnership.

11. Be sure to pass on good words to the principal when the regular education teacher is doing good work with your students.

12. Reward the teachers who work well with special needs students—examples include a thank you note, a new pen, stickers they can give their students—and encourage the teachers who need assistance.

WHERE DOES THE SPECIAL EDUCATOR FIND SUPPORT?

Support is out there!

> *It's okay to ask for help. Don't hesitate to ask your questions. Being organized and seeking resources are the key to survival.*
>
> *Barbara Danoff*

1. Find those notebooks from your methods courses. It's not time to put them away, but time to begin applying strategies.

2. Your administrator/secretary can be of support to first-year teachers. The principal can assist in setting up positive communication between special and regular educators.

3. Call on fellow special educators.

4. Participate in inservice programs.

5. Go back to college: Ask professors for advice and guidance.

6. Use your colleagues as a support system.

7. The education of special education students is a shared responsibility. Work with the regular educator to problem-solve.

8. Use CEC as a resource—especially their quarterly journal called *TEACHING Exceptional Children (TEC)*.

9. Attend conferences and conventions to learn new strategies. Use them as opportunities to discover others who are in similar teaching situations and trade ideas.

10. Get involved in the local CEC chapter. Call CEC's Department of Member and Unit Services for a contact at the nearest local chapter.

Be Kind to Yourself and Enjoy

I would tell a first-year teacher to relax, enjoy your students and admit to yourself that the first year is going to sometimes be rough but that you are going to take the mistakes and criticism in stride and work to better yourself. It can be fun!
Janet Witte

STRESS MANAGEMENT TIPS FOR TEACHERS

Beginning a new school year is always stressful for any teacher; as a novice, it seems there are even more things to worry about. It is important to your physical and mental health to keep a handle on the stressors in your new environment.

When stress does occur, it is important to recognize and deal with it. As you begin to understand more about how stress affects you, you will discover effective ways to ease the tension. Some ideas to keep in mind for addressing or reducing stress follow:

1. Mix relaxation with your daily teaching responsibilities. After pushing all day, don't push more when you come home. Develop a relaxed spirit within yourself. Keep a balance in your life—friends, family, work, community, and self.
2. Make a list of relaxing activities and plan to participate in them at least three times each week. Schedule fun!
3. As you shower in the morning, visualize your routine for that day.
4. Wear clothes that are comfortable.
5. Plan to arrive at school at least 15 minutes before you are required to be there.
6. Find humor in stressful situations. Your students will appreciate and learn from your ability to laugh when things don't go exactly as planned.
7. Anticipate your students' reactions to lessons and plan accordingly.
8. Get it off your chest. Talk about your day with a caring friend, but avoid getting caught up in school gossip.
9. If you've had a bad day, plan something relaxing to take your mind off the day's events: Read a book, exercise, meet a friend for dinner. Then, after you've recaptured your perspective, evaluate the day's events to determine what, if anything, could have been done differently.
10. Make a few "emergency" lesson plans for those days when you are absent unexpectedly or when your other plans fall through.
11. Prepare for the next morning before you leave school each day.
12. Shun the Superman/Superwoman image—don't expect more of yourself than is

realistic. And, don't expect yourself to immediately discover successful strategies for teaching *all* of your students—it takes time.

13. When in doubt, ask questions.
14. Get help with the tasks you don't fully understand.
15. Designate one specific place for your keys at home and at school.
16. Prepare to get all of the illnesses that your students pass around.
17. Say "no" when your gut feeling tells you to.
18. Don't rely on your memory. Write down all appointments and arrangements made with students, parents, etc.
19. Make lists of things to do today, this week, this quarter, etc., to help you keep your priorities straight.
20. Keep a list of things you would like to do next year or try a different way.
21. There is a fine line between caring about the kids and getting too emotionally involved with them—be careful.
22. Have fun! This is what you've been trained to do! And yes, it does get easier—experience is a great teacher.

NETWORKING

Beginning a new teaching position can seem like as much work as reinventing the wheel if you try to do everything yourself. Therefore, use all the resources available to you—it will help you be more effective and ease your stress.

> *One situation in which I found myself for which I wasn't really prepared was having to deal with irate regular educators. You can state laws and definitions all you like, but when a teacher wants a problem student out of his or her classroom, no college class will tell you how to change his or her mind. To address this, I gained the support of the principal, special education director, counselor and other teachers. A special educator must educate regular education teachers on how to deal with students in special education as well as with borderline students.*
>
> **Bob Hitt**

1. Meet with your supervisor or department chairperson as early as possible to find out exactly what is expected and required of you.
2. Next, explore your classroom to see what materials you have and determine what you think you will need. Seek advice from other special education teachers in your building.
3. Seek out other new teachers in your building; these are great people with whom to network. Although they may not know much more about the workings of the school than you do, they are struggling with the same orientation process.
4. Find out what materials and/or services your local education agency has available and how you can utilize them.

5. Stay in touch with your college classmates; they can be invaluable sources of ideas and support.

6. Learn your district's policy on attending conferences throughout the year. Then choose carefully so you gain full benefit from the speakers and presentations you hear. After attending a conference, write a synopsis of the presentations to share with your colleagues.

7. Share your ideas and thoughts freely with your colleagues, keeping in mind that others may or may not agree with you.

8. Attend CEC chapter meetings. You will meet people who can be good resources.

9. Encourage the support and involvement of parents. They can be a helpful resource.

10. Volunteer to serve as a club sponsor—you will get to work with students in a non-academic setting.

11. Enroll in a graduate education course. Expand your knowledge base. Learning is like scaffolding. Don't feel like you have to know everything at once. Work on building a solid foundation.

12. Read extensively in professional journals.

13. No one understands what it is like to be a teacher, except a teacher. As a result, be kind to your colleagues and take care of one other.

STRESS IN CHILDREN

Be aware that your students will also experience stress at school. Moreover, a student will often take stress out on the person he feels secure with or in the environment where he feels secure (it's really a backward compliment!).

> *One of my students was working on making change up to $1.00. I spent months trying a variety of teaching approaches. We both were just about to put the concept away for awhile, when something clicked and she understood! We jumped up and down and the next day we had an "I can make change" party.*
> *Barbara Danoff*

To reduce stress for your students, be aware that exceptional students need:

1. As much *certainty* and *consistency* as possible;
2. To be surrounded by *positive* people;
3. Help to face *change*;
4. Lessons in dealing with stress;
5. Help in coming to terms with *visible evidence* of their disability;
6. Help in coping with *invisible* handicaps;
7. A chance to help others understand; and
8. Help in setting goals for themselves.

PRACTICE POSITIVE STRESS MANAGEMENT IN YOUR CLASSROOM

If you sense your students are feeling quite a bit of stress, you may want to tell them the following to help them relax.

Picture in your mind a bright red marble lying beside your right foot. Wiggle your toes for a minute. Feel your toes as they move about inside your shoe. Now pick up that red marble with your toes. Curl your toes slowly over it and squeeze. Now you have the red marble tight in your toes. Feel how strong those toe muscles are. Don't let any other part of your body help. Your toes must hold the marble all by themselves. Open your toes and let the marble go. Let your toes relax completely.

Now tighten your leg muscles. Can you squeeze them harder than your toe muscles? Tense your leg muscles as though you are getting ready to start a race. The race isn't quite ready to begin, so you can relax for a minute. Now the other runners are getting into position. Get ready. Tighten your leg muscles, ready to push off. Pull them tight. Ready? They have just signaled that the race has been postponed. You can relax. Let your leg muscles go completely loose.

Now think about your hands and arms. Picture a chinning bar in your mind. Imagine you're putting your hands on the bar and taking a good hold. Feel your hands tighten and your arm muscles work as you begin to pull yourself up. Make your arm muscles pull even tighter. Feel how hard they are when they're pulling. That's fine. Now drop down to the ground. Let your arms and hands relax. Doesn't it feel good to let your arms sag and go limp?

Now concentrate on your stomach. Feel it rise and fall as you breathe. Pull in your stomach muscles. Pull them so tight that it seems as though they will touch your backbone. Now relax and let your stomach muscles go loose. Just let them sag. See how good it feels when your muscles relax?

It is time to let your face do some of the work. Think about your face. Your forehead is smooth, your cheeks and mouth are relaxed. Put your head back and just relax for a moment. Now picture in your mind a small leak in the ceiling above your head. Notice that a drop of water is about to fall directly on your face. When it does, you must scrunch up your eyes and tighten all of your face muscles. Your cheeks will push up toward your eyes, your mouth will close tightly. Ready? Here comes that drop right onto your face—plop! Now relax those tight muscles. Let your cheeks go loose. Relax your mouth and jaw.

You may open your eyes now. Do you see how you can talk to different parts of your body and tell them when to tighten and when to relax? Doesn't it feel good when you can tell your muscles to let go, to loosen?

An important lesson I learned was to not be too hard on myself. Everything will get done in time. Students won't be permanently damaged if a lesson doesn't go just the way you planned. Let the students know that you are human. And, don't try to go it alone. Find someone that you trust and talk to them...a lot. Share the feelings of frustration and, more importantly, the good stuff that happens.

Theresa Trimm

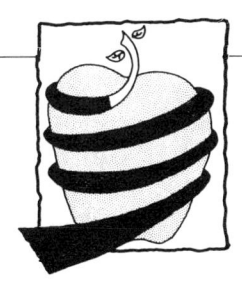

Think About It

During my first year of teaching, I learned to ask questions about policies, procedures, regular education curriculum, etc., and not try to act like I knew it all—because I didn't.
　　　　　　　　　　　　　　　　Janet Witte

6

This chapter describes some "situations" that you may find yourself in during your teaching career. We hope that by giving you a chance to think about them now, you will feel more comfortable responding if you find yourself in such a situation. As you think about how you would respond, keep in mind that there is no "right" answer—only many alternatives. If possible, talk these over with another teacher.

SITUATIONS TO THINK ABOUT

1. John has been a severe behavior problem. He has been suspended from school before for hitting other students, kicking a teacher, and smashing windows. He is a big fellow, and most students and quite a few teachers are afraid of him.

    You have only had a few minor problems with John. Today, however, he seems quite irritated. You have been ignoring him and have not even encouraged him to do any work.

    You are handing back tests that your class did yesterday. John got a score of 38. One of the students asks you what the highest test score was and you say, "The highest score was 96 and the lowest was 38." John says softly, but loudly enough so everyone can hear, "Why you %&*($!" You look at John and say, "Don't you talk like that in this class!" He jumps out of his seat with teeth clenched and fists raised and starts walking toward you. What are your options? Which option will you choose? Why?

2. Your school has been plagued by acts of vandalism lately. Last week your principal asked all faculty members to keep a sharp eye out for vandals. Three teachers per day have been assigned to walk the halls during lunch period. Today is your day.

    You're walking alone down a hallway at the far end of your building. No one else is nearby and all is quiet. Suddenly you hear a loud crash coming from one of the student restrooms and some muffled cheering.

    You cautiously open the restroom door. Inside you find 4 very guilty looking students who appear to be shocked by your intrusion. One of the stall walls has been pulled from the restroom wall and is laying on the floor. You say, "OK, let me have your names." The 4 students say, "No way!" So you say, "OK, come with me then." Again they refuse. What will you do next?

3. Your self-contained class for multiply handicapped children is housed, along with two others, at one end of an elementary school. Because of the special needs of your children, you and two other teachers are not assigned to bus duty, recess duty, or school program responsibilities. As you three walk in, slightly late, to a teachers' meeting you overhear a group of teachers talking about you. "They really have it easy, you know . . . . " You feel they are envious because you have few children and school duties. What are your options? How do you handle the situation?

4. One day last week you telephoned Mrs. Tyler to let her know that her daughter Beth (one of your students) had not been turning in her homework recently. Mrs. Tyler assured you that she would see that Beth had her homework done every day.

   The day after you telephoned, Mrs. Tyler called to let you know that Beth would be out for a few days because of illness. As you are getting ready for your first period class, you see Beth standing in the doorway of your classroom. You ask Beth if she's feeling better. She says yes and then breaks down crying. You go to her and ask her what's wrong. Between sobs she tells you that her mother beat her because of your phone call. Her mother had wanted to keep her out of school because of her bruised face. What are your reactions and feelings? Will you ask Beth for more details? How or will you follow up with Beth? With your principal? With Mrs. Tyler? With community resources?

5. Sheldon is a constant problem. He has been in trouble in school many times and is doing very poorly in his schoolwork.

   Cigarettes are not allowed in your school. Your principal has asked that teachers confiscate any that are found. You are walking across your room to check on a student's work. You glance toward Sheldon and notice that he has a pack of cigarettes in his pocket.

   You walk over to Sheldon and say, "What's in your pocket?" His response is "nothing." You then say, "Let me have them or you are going to the office." Sheldon won't give you the cigarettes, so you say, "Go to the office right now." He won't do that either. Meanwhile, all work in the room has stopped and everyone is watching the conflict. What are you going to do? How will you get the class back on task?

I found myself having to work with a teacher who wouldn't cooperate with me. I attempted several times to work with the teacher—no luck. Finally, the principal helped me out of the situation. She helped me devise a schedule conflict so I had to move my students to another general education room. No one except the principal and I knew the real reason. Now I ask a lot of questions before placing a student with another teacher.

Wendy Haight

---

6. You are a high school learning disabilities specialist and you have been experiencing reasonable success with your students. You are receiving more and more referrals from certain teachers, though. Additionally, teachers seem to be sending you children who have behavior problems rather than learning problems.

You have always accepted these referrals, trying to establish a cooperative atmosphere.

Now you go to one of these teachers to ask if he will accept one of your slow learners in his biology class. He flatly refuses, saying that he is too busy to give individual help to that child. How will you respond? What next steps will you try?

7. The Sanchezes are new in your community and Juan has only been in your classes for 2 weeks. You have never met Mr. Sanchez.

   Ms. Carter, the principal, just called your room and asked you to come to the office. She informed you that Mr. Sanchez was there. You have gone to the office, met Mr. Sanchez, and have taken a seat next to him.

   Ms. Carter explains to you that Mr. Sanchez is concerned about your ability to teach since he doesn't think the information you are presenting in your classes is accurate and up-to-date. Mr. Sanchez states, in very difficult-to-understand English, that this is his major concern. Ms. Carter doesn't come to your defense. She simply asks for your response. What will you say to Mr. Sanchez? How do you feel about Ms. Carter's handling of the situation? What will you say to Ms. Carter?

8. One of your students writes a note to a friend and you pick it up. It contains information that the student wants to kill himself. What do you do?

9. You have evidence that a child is on drugs. What do you do? Do you inform the parents? Your principal? How?

10. You set up a reinforcement contract with one of your student's parents. The student is following through on his part of the contract but the parents are not doing their share. How do you ensure the parents' participation?

11. One of your student's parents dies unexpectedly. How do you help?

12. You hear one of your fellow teachers talking to a student about a confidential matter that involves a special education student. What do you do?

13. After evaluating one of your students, you determine that your classroom is not the most appropriate placement for him. You share your findings with the principal and recommend that he be put in a more appropriate setting. The principal refuses your recommendation and tells you that the student must stay in your classroom. What are your options? Do you do anything else, or do you accept the principal's ruling, although you know it is not the best situation for the student?

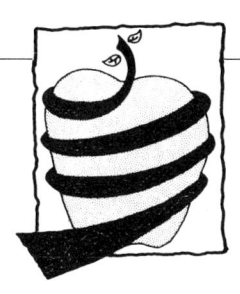

Some Closing Thoughts

One of my fondest memories of my first year of teaching was during the second to last week of school when one of my lowest functioning students was finally able to recognize and write his name, a skill that we had worked on all year. I knew then that I was going to be able to succeed as a teacher and learned not to give up when everything looks bad.

Melissa Moore

As you know, your first year of teaching will be unlike anything you have experienced and nothing will prepare you for all the situations you will encounter. Take heart, though: Your second year and subsequent ones will be different because of the experience you gained in your first year.

Remember, you will have "bad" days during your first year—as well as throughout your career. Bad days don't mean that you've chosen the wrong profession; they simply mean that you're human. "Unload" whatever happens during the day, both the good and the bad, and be ready to start fresh the next day.

Think about keeping a journal during your first year: Include things you would do differently; notes about things that occur that are priceless, humorous, or that you don't want to forget; comments that your students make; or other memories that you want to keep. It would be enjoyable to have these anecdotes to look back on throughout your career.

Finally, we asked a few teachers, "If you could tell a first-year teacher one thing, what would it be?" Their comments provide good closing advice.

(1) Develop a philosophy about your job. Work toward reaching your philosophical goals. (2) Always treat your students and the parents of your students with the highest respect. (3) Don't be a "pal" to your students, be a guide. (4) Try to keep a perspective on the nondisabled population and how your students will fit into the community. (5) Remember you are only one person—sometimes you won't be successful and you need to be ready to call upon others to help students reach their goals. (6) Never stop learning.

Judy Larson, teacher of students who are severely behavior disordered, Washington

Allow/give yourself room for growth, expect constant change, try to stay organized, and use your time to your best advantage.

> Natalie Ward, teacher of students who are emotionally handicapped and educably mentally disabled, Florida

Always speak positively about your students—even in the teacher's lounge. You will hear other teachers speaking negatively about their students, but keep your comments positive. You have to be the PR person for your students—no one else will do it. Also, don't make waves. Don't try to change the system or tell anyone big problems you see within the school. You will have plenty of time for that in the future. Good relationships with administrators and staff are more important.

> Wendy Haight, teacher of students who are learning disabled and educably mentally disabled, Michigan

Maintain your sense of humor. When all the stress and work begin to mount and it seems that things never go your way, laughter really helps.

> Lloyd Nakamura, teacher of students who are gifted and talented, Hawaii

Learn to get along with your fellow teachers and be willing to go the extra mile for the best interests of your students.

> Eleanor Coffield, teacher of students who are speech impaired, Missouri

Emphasize the positive. Teach as you would to a nonhandicapped child; accommodate his disability, yes, but encourage performance to the extent of his ability. Make him proud of each improvement.

> Clarissa Hug, retired teacher, Illinois

Listen to the kids. Sometimes it's really easy to get caught up in paperwork and curriculum guidelines to the point that we forget to really 'listen' to what they tell us.

> Lynette Flight, teacher of students who are learning disabled, Illinois

Be open to suggestions, be alert to cues from fellow teachers, and, above all, develop early in the year a fair, optimistic, consistent approach to managing behavior in the classroom. Most importantly, be open to learning with and about each student to really develop a perspective about students from observation and interaction—not psychological reports.

M. Beth Langley, teacher of students who are multiply handicapped, Florida

Don't try to solve the world's problems, or the school system's problems in one year. Do a few things well, rather than everything half-way. You can create a repertoire of good methods, materials, and practices over several years.

Dawn Carson, teacher of students who are educably mentally disabled, British Columbia

Take care of yourself, both physically and mentally. There is nothing worse than feeling the pressure and stress of teaching and trying to accomplish something when you are sick. You can only be good for your students when you are good for yourself.

Theresa Trimm, teacher of students who are emotionally handicapped and learning disabled, Michigan

Best of luck and enjoy!

Join CEC Today!

The Council for Exceptional Children (CEC) is the largest professional organization committed to improving educational outcomes for individuals with exceptionalities. CEC accomplishes its worldwide mission on behalf of special educators and others working with children with exceptionalities by advocating for appropriate government policies; setting professional standards; providing continuing professional development; and assisting professionals to obtain conditions and resources necessary for effective professional practice.

CEC Membership Benefits

- **Journals and Resources**
  Receive *TEACHING Exceptional Children* and *Exceptional Children* included with your membership. Access the most complete collection of special education information in the world. Enjoy member discounts—up to 30%—on products and services.

- **Career Development**
  Professional Networking
  Improve your knowledge and skills. Network with colleagues for ongoing support. Attend CEC professional development programs at special member rates. Join CEC's Divisions—providing additional focus to a wide variety of aspects of special education. Each division develops professional programs and publications in response to areas of particular need and specialization.

- **Security and Savings**
  CEC membership includes the protection of hard-to-find professional liability, major medical, and term life insurance plans at group rates. Apply for a major credit card at no annual fee the first year.

Join Today and Save!

- Annual subscription to: *Exceptional Children*   (value $48)
  and *TEACHING Exceptional Children*   (value $32)
- Convention registration discounts   (value $45)
- Workshops discounts   (value $20)
- Publication and product discounts   (value 30%)

Plus! Automatic membership in your provincial or state federation.

Call 1-800-8456-CEC

The Council for Exceptional Children
1920 Association Drive
Reston, VA 22091-1589

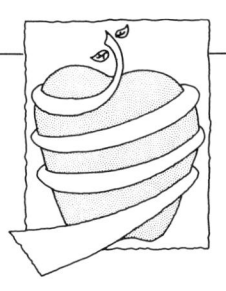

Information Resources Available from CEC

Appendix

Journals

TEACHING Exceptional Children: This quarterly journal includes state-of-the-art classroom methods for the practitioner and articles on programs and practices proven to boost teacher effectiveness. Updates on new materials and latest news are included in each issue.

Exceptional Children: This is *the* journal for special education professionals and is published six times annually. It contains comprehensive, thoroughly researched, in-depth articles on the development and education of exceptional children.

ERIC Clearinghouse on Disabilities and Gifted Education

The ERIC Clearinghouse is the most complete and comprehensive collection of literature on special education information in the world. CEC has housed the Clearinghouse since its inception in 1966.

Professional Materials, Services, and Career Development

Teaching aids, professional materials and research services are all available—and at member discounts. CEC is the standard setter for special education teacher preparation, classroom practices, and certification. The annual international convention features 700 professional programs. Topical conferences, symposia, and workshops are held by CEC and by its chapters, federations, and divisions. Teacher Effectiveness Academies deliver advanced skill training to local practitioners and their supervisors.

Names of Other CEC Members in Your Area

CEC's Department of Member and Unit Services can provide information about the local chapter closest to you so that you can become involved in a local network of members. For membership information call 1-800-8456-CEC.

And Much, Much More

If you have a question, are looking for a particular material, or are searching for some resource, call CEC at 703-264-9474 and see if we can help.

NOTES

NOTES

CEC TEACHER RESOURCES

Tough to Reach, Tough to Teach: Students with Behavior Problems

by Sylvia Rockwell

Through the use of anecdotes, the author prepares teachers for the shock of abusive language and hostile behavior in the classroom. This book will allow you to have a plan for meeting the challenges of teaching these students more effective ways to communicate. Provides many practical management strategies for defusing and redirecting disruptive behavior.

No. P387.   1993.   106 pp.   ISBN 0-86586-235-4

Regular Price $20.00   CEC Member Price $14.00

Integrating Transition Planning into the IEP Process

by Lynda L. West, Stephanie Corbey, Arden Boyer-Stephens, Bonnie Jones, Robert J. Miller, Mickey Sarkees-Wircenski

Shows how to incorporate transition planning into the IEP process. Helps students become self-advocates. Describes skills needed for employment, community living, postsecondary education, and leisure activities. Includes three sample IEPs.

No. P386.   1992.   78 pp.   ISBN 0-86586-222-2

Regular Price $15.70   CEC Member Price $11.00

Survival Guide for the First-Year Special Education Teacher

by Julie Berchtold Carballo, Mary Kemper Cohen, Barbara Danoff, Maureen Gale, Joyce M. Meyer, and Christine-Louise Elizabeth Orton

Tips for new teachers to start you off on the right foot. Tells how to get organized, how to get to know the students, how to get along with co-workers and parents, and how to take care of yourself.

No. P335.   1990.   45 pp.   ISBN 0-86586-196-X

Regular Price $11.40   CEC Member Price $8.00

Resourcing: Handbook for Special Education Resource Teachers

by Mary Yeomans Jackson

Gives special education teachers the help they need to fill new roles outside the self-contained classroom. Shows how to be the best resource to other teachers, administrators, community agencies, students, and parents. Written by a practitioner who knows how to make it work.

No. P366.   1992.   64 pp.   ISBN 0-86586-219-2

Regular Price $11.40   CEC Member Price $8.00

Prices may change without notice.

Send orders to: The Council for Exceptional Children, Dept. K30850, 1920 Association Drive, Reston, VA 22091-1589. 703/620-3660 Voice/TDD.

Quantity discounts based on regular prices for orders of the same title shipped to one address are as follows: 10–49 copies, 20%; 50–99 copies, 25%. For orders over 100 copies, please call 703-264-9468 for special pricing.